SHINE THEORY

GUIDE TO JEWELLERY STYLING

RASHI SHARMA

Thank you for your unwavering faith and encouragement to everyone who believed in me.

• • •

A heartfelt and special thanks to my father, whose dream of seeing me publish a book has been a guiding light throughout this journey. Your vision continues to inspire me every day.

• • •

To my most supportive husband, whose strength, love, and constant encouragement turned this dream into a reality — this would not have been possible without you.

• • •

And to my most loving son, who stood by his mommy with patience, pride, and pure love as she brought this book to life, you are my greatest motivation.

• • •

This book is for you, with all my heart.

Contents

About The Author

Rashi Sharma never set out to become a jewellery stylist. In fact, if you had met her a decade ago, she was just a young woman captivated by the beauty of heritage karigari and modern minimalism—scribbling designs in notebooks and stringing together ideas with hope in her heart.

Today, she is the founder of **Zayn Luxury Jewellery**, a brand she named after her son, Zayn—her greatest source of inspiration and joy. What started as a dream built from her living room table has grown into a beloved boutique and exclusive styling studio in South Delhi. But through all the growth, one thing has never changed: her deep, personal connection to every woman she works with.

With over 10 years of experience in the jewellery world, Rashi has styled thousands of clients—each with a unique story, a different hesitation, and a sparkle waiting to be unlocked. She has stood behind countless dressing mirrors, gently helping brides find the necklace, reassuring first-timers who weren't sure if bold earrings were "too much," and celebrating that quiet moment when someone looks in the mirror and finally sees their full self—radiant and real.

Her style philosophy is simple: jewellery should feel like you. It should never overpower you, only enhance the brilliance that's already there. Whether it's a dainty pendant or a dramatic cuff, Rashi believes every piece has a soul—and when matched with the right person, it comes to life.

This book, Shine Theory, is Rashi's love letter to every woman who has ever felt unsure about how to wear jewellery, who has played it safe, or who has thought, "I love it, but I don't know if I can pull it off." She wrote this for you—to guide, to reassure, and to remind you that confidence isn't found in a box; it's found in how you choose to wear what's already yours.

Known for her minimalist personal style and her love for quiet elegance, Rashi travels the world curating collections that are rich in craftsmanship, character, and charm. Every piece she selects carries a story—just like the women she styles.

Rashi Sharma isn't just designing jewellery. She's helping women rediscover themselves—**one beautiful, thoughtful piece at a time.**

Introduction

"Jewellery has the power to be the one little thing that makes you feel unique."
— Elizabeth Taylor

Ten years ago, when I launched my jewellery brand in the heart of Delhi, I thought I understood style. But it wasn't until I worked one-on-one with hundreds of women—brides preparing for the biggest day of their lives, working professionals dressing for boardrooms, fashion lovers curating the perfect festive look—that I discovered a truth far deeper than trends: jewellery is personal magic.

Back then, I used to see jewellery as the cherry on top—an afterthought to complete a look. But that changed the moment I began styling real people. I watched how a single piece—be it a pair of delicate hoops or a bold choker—could shift someone's energy. It wasn't just an accessory. It was **transformation in metal and stone.**

Suddenly, I saw things differently.The way earrings framed a face. The way a layered necklace drew the eye and elevated a simple kurta.The way a bride's smile widened when the right maang tikka completed her glow.That's when it clicked for me: jewellery isn't the finishing touch—it's the starting point.It sets the mood. It tells your story before you say a word. It adds that final polish that makes people turn their heads. And the best part? You don't need to be a fashion expert to wear it well—you just need the right guidance.That's why I wrote Shine Theory.Because I've seen the hesitation when someone loves a piece but says, "I don't know how to wear this."I've seen people stick to the same studs every day—not out of choice, but out of habit.I've heard the excitement in their voice when they finally try something new and feel amazing doing it.

This book is your styling companion—the guide I wish I had when I was starting out. I'll walk you through the art of layering, mixing metals, matching pieces to your neckline, face shape, outfit, and occasion. Whether you're dressing for a casual day or a celebration that means everything, I'll help you unlock the power of the perfect piece.Each page is filled with real-life styling tips, stories from my journey, and practical advice that you can apply instantly. This is about more than jewellery—it's about discovering your confidence, creativity, and sparkle.

So open your jewellery box with fresh eyes. That dainty chain? It's elegance.Those bold earrings? They're attitude.Your favourite ring? It's your anchor.In Shine Theory, we're not just styling jewellery.
We're styling you—your story, your vibe, your shine.

CHAPTER I

The Power of Jewellery in Personal Styling

"You won't believe what happened on my wedding day"

Every girl grows up dreaming of her wedding day — the moment she steps into a new life, feeling like the most beautiful version of herself. I had imagined that moment a hundred times. I planned everything down to the finest detail: a breathtaking Indian outfit, a world-class makeup artist, an elegant hairstyle... everything to make me feel perfect.

Except, life had other plans.

The only thing I hadn't seen or selected myself was the jewellery. My father had insisted, with a quiet smile, "Let me take care of that." He said he'd bring it to the salon on the day itself. I trusted him — he always knew what was best for me. Still, a part of me was anxious, not knowing what I would wear with my dream outfit.

Then the big day arrived, and it started falling apart.

My outfit didn't fit as it should. The salon team had to step in and fix it on the spot. My hair turned oily, and the hairstyle I had envisioned didn't work. The makeup artist worked her magic, but the emotions caught up with me as I sat in the chair. The realization that I was leaving my home, my parents, my childhood behind — it hit me like a wave. I cried, not just a little, but the kind of tears that come from deep within. And with those tears came something I never expected — breakouts. Pimples on the one day I was supposed to glow.

I looked in the mirror and felt broken. This wasn't how I had pictured myself on my wedding day. Everything felt off, like a dream slipping through my fingers.

And then... my father walked in.

He held a small box — not just any box, but one that carried his love, his hopes, and his belief in me. He had handpicked every single piece of jewellery as a surprise. When the makeup artist helped me put it on, something shifted.

The necklace settled around my neck like it was always meant to be there. The earrings framed my face and drew attention away from the imperfections. The bangles sparkled with every movement, almost like they were dancing in celebration.

In that moment, all the chaos faded.

The outfit mishap didn't matter. The hair didn't matter. The pimples didn't matter. Because that jewellery, chosen by my father with so much love, transformed everything. Not just how I looked, but how I felt. I saw myself in the mirror and, for the first time that day, I smiled. I felt radiant. I felt complete.

That day, I realized something powerful:
Jewellery isn't just a part of your styling — it's an emotion.
It carries stories, love, strength, and magic. And sometimes, it becomes the anchor that holds you steady when everything else falls apart.

My wedding look wasn't perfect, but the moment I wore that jewellery, it became unforgettable.

That day, I realized something that will stay with me forever: **jewellery isn't just an accessory—it's a statement.** *It has the power to transform not just how you look, but how you feel.*

CHAPTER II

The 7 Mistakes of Jewellery Styling

"Identify and avoid the most common jewellery styling errors"

1. Over-accessorising

Wearing too many pieces at once can create a cluttered, distracting look. Jewellery should enhance your outfit, not compete with it.

Tip: Choose one statement piece and keep the rest minimal for balance.

"Less, But Luxe: A Beach Wedding Story"

As a jewellery stylist, I've always believed that minimalism isn't about lack—it's about impact. It's the quiet confidence of knowing what works without trying too hard. But as much as I live by that rule, convincing others, especially clients used to equating 'more' with 'festive', hasn't always been easy.

One such instance became a turning point for me. I met a girl who was not only stunning but also had this vibrant personality that instantly lit up the room. She was attending a beach wedding—not just any guest, but the bride's closest friend. It was her moment to shine, just not outshine. And I saw potential. We instantly clicked, and today, she's not just a memory but a dear friend.

But back then, we were on opposite ends of the jewellery philosophy. She loved accessorising—layered necklaces, chunky earrings, stacked bangles—the works. She believed it added glamour, celebration, and personality. And yes, I understood where she was coming from. After all, it's a wedding, and she wanted to look her best. But a beach wedding is a delicate canvas. The setting already gives you the breeze, the sun-kissed glow, and the ocean's sparkle. It doesn't need competition.

I explained gently, "When you're unsure about what jewellery to wear, go minimal. It won't fail you." I styled her for one of the functions—a breezy afternoon mehendi by the beach. We went for an elegant pair of statement earrings and skipped everything else. Hair loosely tied, skin glowing, and not a single necklace or bangle to distract. She looked effortless, fresh, and in tune with the setting. Heads turned. Compliments poured in. Not for the jewellery, but for the whole look.

For the rest of the celebrations, she followed her own instincts—layered up again, as she had initially planned. She looked beautiful, of course, but something was missing. The jewellery, though striking, overwhelmed the natural vibe of the beach wedding. It pulled attention in different directions, rather than framing her look. Later, she told me, "You were right. That one day I let you style me, I've never felt more seen. More myself." That moment stayed with me. Because minimalism, when done right, doesn't dull your sparkle—it amplifies your presence. It allows people to see you, not just your jewellery.

Since then, she's trusted me more and even refers to me as "the one who taught me the power of less."

2. Mismatching Jewellery with the Outfit

Not all jewellery works with every outfit. Heavy traditional pieces with modern minimal clothing or vice versa can clash.

Tip: Match the vibe — traditional with ethnic, minimal with modern, bold with evening wear, etc. One of the most important rules in personal styling is ensuring that your jewellery complements your outfit. Not all kinds of jewellery work with every look, and mismatched combinations can take away from even the most beautiful ensembles. A lot of people make the mistake of pairing jewellery without considering the overall vibe. It's not just about wearing what's trendy or expensive — it's about creating harmony between your outfit and accessories . Contrasting thoughtfully can elevate your look, but it has to be intentional. You need to assess the colours, the textures, the neckline, and most importantly, the occasion. What you wear to a wedding, a formal event, or a casual brunch should all be approached differently when it comes to jewellery. At the end of the day, your jewellery should enhance your outfit, not overpower or confuse it. Understanding the vibe, reading the occasion, and selecting pieces that flow together — that's the true art of styling.

3. Clashing Metals -Uncoordinated metals

Mixing too many metal tones — gold, silver, rose gold — without intention can look uncoordinated.

Tip: Stick to one metal or mix them strategically with pieces that are designed to blend.

4. Ignoring Face -Jewellery That Doesn't Complement Your Features

Wearing jewellery that doesn't suit your face shape or body frame can throw off your entire look.

Tip: For example, long earrings flatter round faces, while studs suit angular faces better.

5. Neglecting Occasion-Appropriate Styling -Failing to Match Jewellery to the Occasion

Wearing heavy, ornate pieces to a casual event or minimal jewellery to a grand celebration can feel out of place.

Tip: Always consider the occasion, venue, and time of day when selecting your jewellery

6. Forgetting to Harmonise with Hairstyle -Styling Without Considering the Hair

Jewellery can get hidden or tangled if it doesn't complement your hairstyle.

Tip: Statement earrings shine with tied-up hair, while studs or ear cuffs work well with open hairstyles.

7. Wearing Jewellery that Doesn't Reflect Your Personality- Wearing Pieces That Don't Align With Who You Are

Copying trends without considering your style can make you feel uncomfortable and inauthentic.

Tip: Choose pieces that resonate with you — **confidence is your best accessory**

Mistakes of Jewellery Styling

over accessorising

$\longleftarrow$

Mismatching jewellery with outfit

$\longrightarrow$

Clashing Of metals

$\longleftarrow$

Mistakes of Jewellery Styling

Office look

Neglecting occasions

→

Bun look

Forgetting to harmonize with hairstyle

←

CHAPTER III

Face Shapes and Jewellery Selection

"More Than Just Sparkle: A Jewellery Story"

My friend was the kind of girl who turned heads without trying—big, expressive eyes, a heartwarming smile, and a natural sense of charm.

She loved jewellery. Her Instagram saved folder was full of trending pieces—chunky hoops, layered chokers, bold cuffs, and quirky statement earrings. She bought what she liked, what was in fashion, or what caught her eye at first glance. To her, jewellery was all about making a statement. And she made many—but not always the right ones.

She had a soft, round face, the kind that radiates youthfulness. But she often chose short, wide earrings or choker-style necklaces that cut her neckline and made her face appear even rounder. Sometimes, she'd wear oversized hoops that clashed with her features rather than complementing them. Her jewellery was always pretty on its own, but something about the full look often felt... off.

When we met for a wedding styling consultation, I instantly noticed her love for accessories. She pulled out her collection with pride, saying, "These are all the pieces I love—they're so trendy!" And they were. But as I observed her trying them on, I gently pointed out how some pieces, although beautiful, weren't doing justice to her natural face structure.

I explained how longer, more vertical earrings could elongate her face, how a more delicate necklace could open up her neckline and give her more balance. At first, she hesitated—style is personal, and no one likes being told their favorites might not be their best. But she agreed to let me style her for one event.

We went with long, elegant drop earrings and skipped the heavy necklace she had picked out. Instead, we added a soft shimmer to her collarbone and kept the overall look light. The difference was immediate. Her face looked lifted, her features more defined, and the compliments that evening.

She came to me later with a smile that said it all. "I never knew jewellery could change the way my face looked. I just picked what I liked. But this...

this feels like it suits me."

That day, she didn't just wear jewellery—she owned her look. She learned that style isn't only about trends or what we're drawn to in the moment. It's about understanding what enhances our natural beauty and choosing pieces that bring balance and harmony.

Because the most beautiful jewellery is the kind that doesn't compete with you—it completes you.

• • •

Identify Your Face Shape

Discover how to choose jewellery that complements your unique face shape for a balanced, refined look.

Step 1: Pull Your Hair Back

Tie your hair into a ponytail or use a headband so your face is completely visible. Use a mirror or take a straight-on selfie in natural light.

Step 2: Measure These Four Key Areas (or Just Observe):

If you want to be precise, use a measuring tape. If not, just observe the proportions visually.

Forehead Width:-Measure across the widest part, usually halfway between your eyebrows and hairline.

Cheekbone Width:-Measure from the outer corner of one eye to the other.

Jawline Width:-Measure from the base of your jaw (under your ear) to the middle of your chin. Double it for both sides.

Face Length:-Measure from the center of your hairline to the bottom of your chin.

Step 3: Analyze the Face Shape

Match your measurements and facial features to these common face shapes:

Oval

Features: Forehead slightly wider than the chin, face length longer than width.

Tip: Most styles work well with this balanced shape!

Square

Features: Forehead, cheekbones, and jawline are almost the same width. Strong jawline.

Tip: Go for soft curves to balance sharp angles.

Heart

Features: Forehead is the widest point, chin is narrow or pointed.

Tip: Choose jewellery that adds width to the jawline area.

Round

Features: Cheekbones are the widest part, with a soft jawline and equal face width/length.

Tip: Long earrings or drop styles help elongate the face.

Diamond

Features: High, defined cheekbones with a narrower forehead and chin.

Tip: Try earrings that balance your cheekbones, like studs or wider drops.

Rectangle

Features: Face is longer than it is wide, with straight cheek lines.

Tip: Go for wider earrings or hoops to add volume to the sides.

Considering your face shape when styling jewellery is one of the most overlooked yet impactful steps in achieving a truly harmonious and flattering look. Each face shape has its unique proportions—whether it's a soft round face, a structured square jawline, a heart-shaped silhouette, or an elegant oval. By selecting jewellery that complements these features, you're not just accessorizing—you're enhancing the natural beauty of the face. For instance, long drop earrings can elongate a round face, while soft curved styles can balance out the strong angles of a square face. Similarly, delicate studs can bring attention to a narrow chin on a heart-shaped face, and hoops can add width to longer or oblong face shapes.

When jewellery is chosen without considering face shape, it can unintentionally overpower or clash with your features. A necklace might cut across your neckline awkwardly, or earrings might pull focus away from your eyes rather than highlighting them. But when jewellery is thoughtfully selected, it enhances rather than distracts—it brings balance, draws attention to your best features, and completes your look in a way that feels intentional and effortless.

From a stylist's perspective, taking face shape into account also allows for a more customized, personal experience. It shows a deeper understanding of your beauty and adds a professional touch that builds trust. It helps clients not only look better but feel more confident, knowing their jewellery isn't just trendy—it's tailored. In the end, jewellery should do more than decorate; it should elevate. And choosing pieces that align with your face shape is a powerful step toward that.

Look Book

Face shapes and western jewellery

DIAMOND

RECTANGLE

Heart

Look Book

Face shapes and western jewellery

13

CHAPTER IV

Jewellery and Outfit Harmony

"Discover the art of coordinating jewellery with your outfit"

Jewellery is more than just an accessory — it's a powerful extension of your outfit, and when styled thoughtfully, it can completely elevate your look. One of the most common fashion mistakes is choosing beautiful jewellery that simply doesn't belong with the rest of the outfit. This is where the concept of jewellery and outfit harmony comes in.

Outfit harmony doesn't mean everything has to be perfectly matching — it's more about balance, proportion, and creating a visual flow. A chunky oxidised silver choker might be stunning, but paired with a sleek modern dress, it may feel out of place. On the other hand, delicate gold chains might not do justice to a heavily embroidered lehenga.

To create harmony, you need to start by understanding the essence of your outfit:

Is it traditional or modern?
Is it casual or formal?
Is it minimal or heavily embellished?

Once you know the tone of your clothing, selecting complementary jewellery becomes more intuitive.

Matching the Vibe, Contrast, and Occasion

The secret to perfect jewellery-outfit pairing lies in matching the vibe, not just the colours. For example, a boho maxi dress calls for layered beads or silver oxidised jewellery, while a power suit might demand sleek metal hoops or a bold statement ring. It's about creating a cohesive look where the jewellery feels like it belongs to the same story as your outfit.

Another key to harmony is smart contrast. This doesn't mean clashing — it means choosing jewellery that enhances your outfit by adding dimension. If your outfit is rich in texture or embroidery, go for simpler jewellery to let the clothing shine. Conversely, if your outfit is plain or monochrome, a bold statement piece can bring it to life.

But harmony also requires occasion-awareness. Wearing elaborate jhumkas or chandbalis to a casual brunch might feel out of place, just as minimal studs may not make enough impact at a wedding.

Always think about:

Time of day: Lighter pieces for daytime, bolder for evening.

Event type: Casual, semi-formal, or festive

Cultural or regional norms: Especially important for traditional wear.

Understanding the occasion helps you fine-tune your choices and ensures your jewellery doesn't feel overdone or underwhelming.

• • •

Practical Tips for Achieving Jewellery and Outfit Harmony

Achieving harmony is both an art and a skill, and the more you experiment with combinations, the better your styling instinct becomes. Here are a few practical tips to help you master it:

The color of your outfit plays a key role in how your jewellery stands out or blends in. Choosing the right jewellery based on your outfit's color can elevate your entire look.

- Warm-toned outfits—like reds, oranges, and yellows—pair beautifully with gold jewellery, enhancing the richness of both.
- Cool-toned outfits—like blues, greens, and purples—often work best with silver, platinum, or white gold, bringing out a sleek and sophisticated vibe.
- Neutral outfits, such as black, white, beige, or grey, offer a versatile canvas, allowing bold, colourful, or statement jewellery to shine
- Depending on the effect you want, coordinating or contrasting jewellery tones with your outfit color adds depth, harmony, or a striking focal point.
- Ultimately, being mindful of colour combinations ensures your jewellery enhances your outfit rather than competes with it.

Pay Attention to Outfit Necklines: The shape of your neckline should guide your necklace choice. V-necks work best with pendants that follow the same shape, while strapless tops are perfect for chokers or layered necklaces.

Balance is Key: If your earrings are big and bold, consider skipping the necklace. If you're stacking bangles, go minimal with rings. Don't overload every part of your look.

Fabric Matters: Light fabrics like chiffon or silk pair beautifully with delicate pieces, while heavier fabrics like velvet or brocade can handle bolder jewellery.

Let One Element Lead: If your outfit is the star, let your jewellery support it. If your jewellery is the highlight, keep your outfit simpler to let it shine.

Lastly, always trust your style. Harmony doesn't mean you can't be creative — it means making styling choices that feel complete, balanced, and you. When your jewellery and outfit speak the same language, your entire look resonates with effortless elegance.

• • •

The Importance of Necklines When Choosing Jewellery

When it comes to styling jewellery, especially necklaces and earrings, the neckline of your outfit plays a starring role. While it's easy to fall in love with a beautiful piece of jewellery, pairing it correctly with your outfit's neckline can make all the difference between a perfectly styled look and one that feels off. Understanding how to balance these elements will elevate your appearance and highlight both your jewellery and your clothing in the best light.

Why Necklines Matter:-

The neckline frames your face, neck, and upper chest — areas where most statement jewellery pieces are worn. Choosing the right necklace length and style can:

- Enhance your overall silhouette
- Draw attention to your features (like collarbones, shoulders, or face)
- Balance proportions between jewellery and clothing
- Create harmony between your outfit and accessories

Wearing the wrong piece with a particular neckline can make even the most stunning jewellery feel out of place, compete awkwardly with your outfit.

Matching Jewellery with Neckline Styles

Let's break down some **popular necklines** and how to style jewellery around them:

1. Staight across necklines

Best Jewellery:

- Chokers or short necklaces that hug the neck
- Statement earrings, if you want to skip the necklace

Why: These necklines leave the collarbones and shoulders bare, giving you the perfect canvas to either highlight the neck with a choker or make a statement with bold earrings. Delicate chains also work if you're going for a more minimal look.

2. V-Neck

Best Jewellery:

- Pendants or drop necklaces that mimic the "V" shape
- Layered chains that taper down

Why: V-necklines naturally draw the eye downward, so pairing them with a similarly shaped pendant enhances that visual line. This creates balance and elongates the neck.

3. Round / Crew Neck

Best Jewellery:

- Collar necklaces or short statement pieces
- Chunky chains that sit just on the neckline

Why: Round necklines cover more of the chest area, so the focus shifts upward. A bold necklace that sits just above the neckline adds volume and visual interest without clashing.

4. Scoop Neck

Best Jewellery:

- Layered necklaces or multi-strand pieces
- Pendant necklaces that fill the open space

Why: A scoop neck offers a wider, deeper canvas, making it ideal for layering or showcasing a focal piece. Avoid overly short necklaces as they can feel disconnected from the neckline.

5. Square Neckline

Best Jewellery:

- Geometric or angular pieces that mirror the lines
- Medium-length pendants that fall just above the bust

Why: Square necklines are structured, so jewellery with some edge or shape complements them beautifully. Stay away from rounded pieces that contrast too much with the linear neckline.

6. Halter Neck

Best Jewellery:

- Skip the necklace or go for minimal chains
- Focus on statement earrings

Why: Halter necks create a visually strong shoulder and neck line. Necklaces can interfere with this design, so earrings take centre stage here — think hoops, chandeliers, or even bold studs.

7. High Neck

Best Jewellery:

- Long chains, pendants, or layered necklaces
- Can also pair with bold earrings

Why: With most of the neck and chest covered, long necklaces help elongate your figure. Chunky chains worn over the fabric also look chic and modern.

• • •

Final Tip

Neckline and jewellery styling go hand-in-hand. The right combination enhances your features, complements your outfit, and expresses your style effortlessly. It's not just about matching shapes — it's about creating harmony between fabric, form, and accessories.

Before choosing your jewellery, take a moment to observe your neckline. Ask: What space do I have to work with? What part of me do I want to highlight? With a little intention, you'll find the perfect match that brings your entire look together

Look Book
Neckline Guide

Square

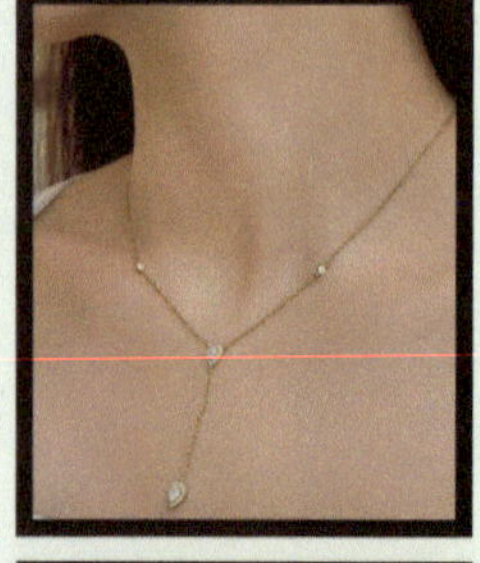

Straight across

Scoop

Sweetheart

Look Book

Neckline Guide

V-neck

High neck

Round neck

Halter

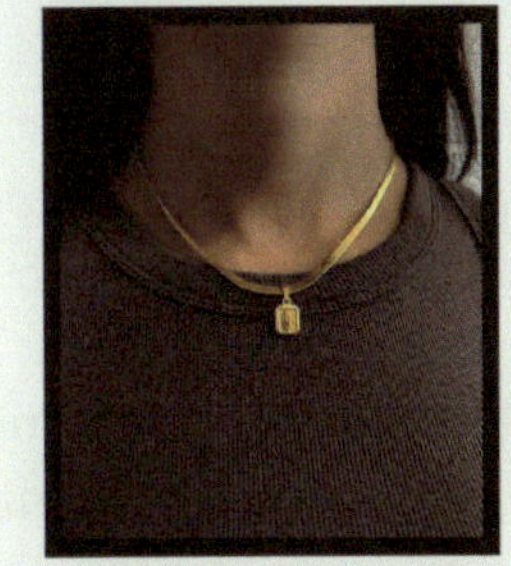

CHAPTER V

The Art of Styling: Bracelets, Bangles & Rings

"The Language of Hands — Why Bracelets, Bangles & Rings Matter"

Our hands are in constant motion — we use them to express, gesture, and connect. That's why what we wear on our wrists and fingers holds more impact than we often realize. Bracelets, bangles, and rings may seem like small accessories, but when styled right, they speak volumes. They can add drama, elegance, tradition, or edge to any look.

Mastering the art of wrist and finger adornments is not about wearing the most jewellery — it's about balance, layering, and intention. These pieces should complement your outfit, reflect your mood or occasion, and enhance the natural beauty of your hands.

Different styles carry different energies:

- Bangles often evoke tradition, celebration, and cultural identity.
- Bracelets lean into contemporary elegance and personality.
- Rings can be symbolic, edgy, or even minimal, but always expressive.

To truly elevate your look, it's important to understand how to mix, match, and layer these pieces without overwhelming your hands or your outfit.

Essential principles for styling bracelets, bangles, and rings:

1. Know the Occasion

Traditional Events: Embrace classic sets of bangles in glass, gold, or kundan. They add rhythm and richness to ethnic wear.

Casual Outings: Try minimalist bracelets or chain-link bangles in metal tones.

Formal or Western Looks: Go for sleek cuffs, charm bracelets, or stacked delicate rings.

2. Balance Your Stack

Avoid overloading both hands with equal weight. For example, if you wear a full stack of bangles on one hand, keep the other hand minimal with just a watch or a single ring.

3. Mix Textures and Materials Smartly

Layer different bracelet types — pair a leather band with a thin gold bangle, or a chunky metal cuff with a delicate chain. The contrast adds dimension. But stay within a color family to avoid looking chaotic.

4. Ring Styling Tips

Statement Rings: Should be worn solo or paired with very subtle other rings.

Stacking Rings: Keep them thin and mix textures or metal tones, but limit to one or two fingers per hand for elegance.

Midi Rings(also known as mid-finger rings or knuckle rings): Great for boho or casual styles, but don't overcrowd — they work best on longer, slender fingers.

5. Coordinate with Your Outfit's Sleeve

Long sleeves or detailed cuffs: Keep wrist jewellery minimal or skip it.

Sleeveless or short sleeves: Go bold — this is your canvas for stacked bangles or chunky bracelets.

Styling your hands isn't just about trends — it's about telling your story. Rings can hold emotional value — engagements, milestones, and heirlooms. Bangles can signify culture, tradition, or festivity. Bracelets often reflect your taste — playful charms, bold cuffs, or minimal chains.

Here's how to make it uniquely yours:

Create Your Signature Stack: Find a go-to combo that feels like your style — maybe a dainty bracelet with a symbolic charm, paired with one ring you never take off. It becomes part of your identity.

Play with Symbolism: Rings with meaningful stones, engraved cuffs, or bangles from special trips — jewellery with stories always stands out.

Confidence is the Finishing Touch: The most important rule in mastering hand jewellery is owning it. Whether you wear a single elegant ring or a full bangle set, when you wear it with confidence, it transforms your presence.

• • •

Quick Tips- Ring Styling

1. Mix & Match

Combine midi rings, statement rings, and thin stacking bands.

Mix metals (gold, silver, rose gold) for a modern, non-uniform look.

Combine shiny and matte, or even add in some textured or hammered rings.

2. Balance Is Key

If you're stacking heavily on one hand, keep the other hand more minimal.

Don't overload every finger; sometimes, just 2–3 fingers with a few rings each look better than full hands.

3. Vary Thickness

Layer thin, dainty rings with one or two bold statement pieces to keep it interesting.

For stacking, start with a base ring and add thinner bands above and below.

4. Consider Nail Polish

Coordinating your nail color with your ring tones can pull everything together.

5. Midi Ring Placement

Wear midi rings on the same fingers as regular rings or on different fingers to build height and visual texture.

They're also great for asymmetrical styles — one on just the pointer or pinky, for example.

• • •

Bracelet Styling Tips

1. Stack It Up

- Layer different types: bangles, cuffs, chains, leather, or beaded styles.
- Play with thickness — wear a chunky cuff with a few thin chain bracelets.

2. Mix Metals and Textures

- Don't be afraid to mix silver, gold, rose gold — just keep the rest of the outfit cohesive.
- Add a pop of color with woven, beaded, or gemstone styles.

3. Watch It

- Bracelets can stack nicely with a watch — just make sure the metals and styles don't clash.
- A minimal watch pairs beautifully with layered chains or delicate bangles.

4. Balance Both Wrists

- Stack one wrist and leave the other bare, or go lighter on one side.
- If you're wearing a lot of rings, consider going light on the bracelets, and vice versa.

5. Match Your Mood or Outfit

- Casual day? Go with leather or fabric wraps.
- Dressed up? Stick to sleek metals or dainty chains with sparkle.

• • •

Bonus Tip: Match Vibe, Not Just Color

- Try to keep your ring and bracelet combo in the same aesthetic category — for example: Boho: stacked rings, earthy stones, woven or beaded bracelets.
- Minimalist: clean lines, dainty metals, one or two thoughtful pieces.
- Edgy: geometric rings, black metals, chunky chain bracelets.

Look Book

Bracelets stacking

Look Book

JEWELLERY STYLING TIPS

Look Book

JEWELLERY STYLING TIPS

CHAPTER VI

Jewellery Styling by Mood and Theme

"The Most Effortless Expression of Mood"

Jewellery is more than adornment — it's a silent yet powerful language of self-expression. With just a ring, a necklace, or a pair of earrings, we communicate who we are, how we feel, and what we want to say to the world — all without speaking a word. Unlike clothing, which often requires planning and coordination, jewellery is the simplest yet most impactful way to shift your vibe instantly.

Feeling bold? Slip on a chunky chain or a statement cuff and you'll radiate confidence before you even say hello. Craving softness or romance? A delicate pearl necklace or rose gold studs gently echo that sentiment. In moments of calm, earthy tones and natural stones align you with serenity. And when you're ready to command a room, glittering chandelier earrings or a radiant cocktail ring amplify your glamour.

What makes jewellery truly special is its ability to adapt. The same pair of hoops can look edgy with leather or playful with a sundress. A layered set of rings can whisper elegance or shout personality, depending entirely on your mood that day.

Jewellery isn't just about beauty — it's about feeling seen, feeling empowered, and feeling like yourself. It's the final touch that transforms an outfit into a message, and a moment into a memory. Whether it's minimal or maximal, classic or quirky, jewellery tells your story — one piece at a time.

So the next time you're deciding what to wear, don't just think about how you want to look — think about how you want to feel. Your mood already knows.

Let Your Jewellery Do The Talking.
1. The Power Look (Professional & Confident)
Mood: Ambitious, Polished, Assertive
Occasions: Work, Presentations, Meetings, Interviews
Must-Haves:

- Minimalist Stud Earrings: Diamond or pearl studs add subtle elegance without being distracting.
- Sleek Chain Necklace: A fine gold or silver chain with a small pendant adds interest without overstatement.
- Structured Bracelet or Cuff: Clean, bold lines work well here — nothing too ornate.
- Statement Watch: Combining form and function, and adds a professional edge.

Styling Tip: Stick to clean metals — gold, silver, or rose gold — and avoid overly dangly or noisy pieces your jewelry should reflect confidence, not compete with your presence.

2. The Romantic Look (Soft, Feminine & Dreamy)

- Mood: Graceful, Elegant
- Occasions: Dates, Garden Parties, Weddings

Must-Haves:

- Pearl Accessories: Classic pearls are timeless and add a delicate, romantic charm.
- Floral-Inspired Rings: Think petal motifs, vine designs, or dainty gemstone clusters.
- Drop Earrings with Soft Stones: Rose quartz, moonstone, or opals pair beautifully with flowy fabrics.
- Layered Chains: Fine gold chains with heart or locket pendants add a dreamy, vintage flair.

Styling Tip: Go for soft metals (rose gold is perfect), and use layering to create a gentle cascading effect that complements flowing outfits and soft colors.

3. The Edgy Look (Bold and Statement-Making)

- Mood: Strong, Expressive, Fearless
- Occasions: Concerts, Night Out, Streetwear Shoots

Must-Haves:

- Chunky Chain Necklaces: The bolder, the better. Layer or wear solo for impact.
- Geometric or Asymmetrical Earrings: Sharp lines or mismatched pairs amp up the drama.
- Stacked Rings: Mix black metals, skull designs, or statement signets for a vibe.
- Leather or Cuff Bracelets: Add texture and contrast with metal studs or charms.

Styling Tip: Black, gunmetal, and oxidized silver give off an effortlessly cool edge. Don't be afraid to go asymmetrical or layer multiple bold pieces.

4. The Glam Look (Elegant, Chic & Party-Ready)

- Mood: Glamorous, Sparkly, Attention-Grabbing
- Occasions: Weddings, Events, Parties, Red Carpet

Must-Haves:

- Chandelier Earrings or Hoops: Crystals or cubic zirconia catch the light for max impact.
- Statement Necklace or Choker: Perfect for off-shoulder or deep neckline dresses.
- Cocktail Ring: A large gemstone or crystal ring draws attention and adds a luxe vibe.
- Tennis Bracelet: A slim line of sparkling stones that adds subtle glam to your wrist.

Styling Tip: Balance is key — if you're wearing a bold necklace, tone down the earrings and vice versa. Metallic tones like rose gold and champagne gold are particularly luxe.

5. The Boho Look (Earthy, Laid-Back & Artistic)

- Mood: Free-Spirited, Natural, Creative
- Occasions: Festivals, Beach Days, Casual Outings

Must-Haves:

- Layered Beaded Necklaces: Natural stones, shells, and charms add texture and color.
- Midi Rings and Toe Rings: These quirky additions feel effortlessly cool and relaxed.
- Feather or Tassel Earrings: Lightweight and playful — perfect for movement.
- Stacked Bracelets: Woven, wooden, or beaded bracelets give that carefree touch.

Styling Tip: Mix natural textures like wood, leather, and stone with metals. The more eclectic the better — boho is all about the mix, not the match.

CHAPTER VII

Occasion-Based Jewellery Styling Tips

"When it comes to accessorizing, context is everythin"

The jewellery that feels perfect for a beach brunch may feel out of place at a formal gala. Tailoring your jewellery choices to the occasion ensures that your overall look feels intentional, polished, and appropriate. Below is your go-to guide for choosing the right pieces — whether you're heading to a coffee date or walking into a black-tie affair.

1. Casual Outings (Brunch, Coffee Dates, Shopping Trips)
Mood: Effortless, relaxed, fun
Jewellery Tips:

- Opt for dainty necklaces, stacked rings, or small hoops.
- Add a bit of personality with layered bracelets, birthstone charms, or boho-inspired midi rings.
- Avoid anything too heavy or sparkly — keep it fresh and low-key.

Best Materials: Sterling silver, rose gold, beads, natural stones
Pair With: T-shirts, denim, casual dresses, flowy tops

2. Travel and vacation
Mood: Comfortable, fuss-free, easygoing
Jewellery Tips:

- Choose water-friendly materials like resin, acrylic, or fabric-based pieces.
- Try shell necklaces, anklets, or woven bracelets.
- Keep it light — both literally and visually — since comfort and ease matter most.
- Choose lightweight earrings, resin bangles, or beaded necklaces that won't tangle or feel heavy.
- Layered bracelets or chokers work well with sundresses and swimsuits.
- Avoid expensive or sentimental jewellery when travelling — opt for fun, replaceable styles.

Style Tip: Stick to one or two versatile pieces that go with everything. A shell choker or evil eye bracelet is perfect for coastal vibes, while gemstone studs suit tropical dinners.

Best Materials: Shells, wood, enamel, rope, silicone

Pair With: Swimwear, cover-ups, maxi dresses, kaftans

3. Work or Office Events

Mood: Professional, polished, poised

Jewellery Tips:

- Stick to minimalist pieces: small studs, thin bracelets, and delicate chains.
- A classic watch or a subtle pendant necklace can add structure to your outfit.
- Avoid noisy bangles or overly flashy items that can be distracting.

Best Materials: Gold, silver, pearls, fine gemstones

Pair With: Blazers, tailored shirts, sheath dresses, monochrome outfits

4. Social Events & Parties

Mood: Glamorous, eye catching, expressive, confident

Jewellery Tips:

- Go for statement earrings, chunky rings, or a bold necklace.
- Choose one statement piece and let it shine, keeping the rest of your accessories complementary.
- Add sparkle, shimmer, or a pop of color to match the fun vibe.
- Bold earrings or necklaces can completely transform a black dress or jumpsuit.
- For club nights or fashion-forward events, layered chains, statement cuffs, or asymmetrical earrings add personality.
- For cocktail parties, gemstone rings and crystal-encrusted pieces work beautifully.

Choose either a statement necklace or statement earrings — not both. Unless you're going full maximalist, balance is essential.

5. Festive look

Mood: Traditional, proud, vibrant, respectful

Jewellery Tips:

- Choose culturally appropriate or inspired jewellery (like jhumkas, maang tikka, or kadas).
- Go ornate if the event calls for it, but ensure it complements your outfit, not competes with it.
- If attending as a guest, opt for mid-level glam — dressy, but not bridal-level.
- Best Materials: Gold, antique finish, enamel, polki, kundan
- Choose classic pieces that carry cultural significance (such as heirlooms, regional designs, or symbols of achievement).
- Pearls, gold chains, or enamel bangles are great choices.

Style Tip: Go for elegance with meaning. Jewellery with personal or family history adds emotional depth to the celebration.

6. Romantic Dates or Intimate Dinners

Mood: Soft, sensual, elegant

Jewellery Tips:

- Choose delicate pendants, soft gemstone rings, or elegant drop earrings.
- Subtle sparkle goes a long way — think rose gold, dainty chains, or a single locket necklace.
- Let the jewellery reflect your personality and complement your look without overpowering it.

Best Materials: Rose gold, moonstone, opal, fine chains

Pair with: Off-shoulder tops, silk blouses, dresses with romantic details

7. Weddings and Celebrations

Goal: Elegant, festive, respectful of the occasion

Jewellery Strategy:

- If you're wearing traditional attire, go for jhumkas, kundan sets, or mang tikka (for South Asian or cultural events).
- For Western-style weddings, opt for pearls, diamond studs, or a sparkling necklace depending on your outfit's neckline.
- Avoid upstaging the bride. Keep it graceful and refined, unless you're part of the bridal party and expected to match the theme.

Style Tip: If your outfit has embellishment (like sequins or lace), let your jewellery be simple. If your outfit is sleek, your accessories can go bold.

8. Spiritual or Mindful Events
Goal: Grounded, natural, intentional
Jewellery Strategy:

- Choose jewellery made from crystals, healing stones, or natural materials.
- Lotus motifs, chakra bracelets, or simple mala beads complement yoga sessions or meditative spaces.
- Stay away from heavy metals or flashy styles.

Style Tip: Choose pieces that feel meaningful — birthstones, engraved charms, or spiritual symbols — as they enhance both style and significance.

• • •

Final Tip

Your jewellery should never feel like an afterthought. When chosen with intention, it enhances your presence, matches your mood, and fits the setting perfectly. Whether it's a laid-back brunch or a formal ceremony, let your jewellery echo the energy of the occasion — it's your silent stylist, storyteller, and signature.

Every occasion is an opportunity to express a different side of yourself. By aligning your jewellery choices with the mood, setting, and purpose of the event, you ensure your accessories don't just look good — they feel right. Let your jewellery be your finishing touch, your signature flair, and your storyteller.

"Styling inspiration with simple visuals to help you pick the perfect jewellery for every occasion."

Western jewellery according to different occasions

Date Look

Neckchain

Bracelet stack

Travel Look

Neckchain

Bracelet stack

Western jewellery according to different occasions

Brunch Look

Earrings

Bracelet stack

Office Look

Neckchain

Bracelet stack

Western jewellery according to different occasions

Party Look

Neckchain

Earrings

Spritual Look

Neckchain

Bracelet stack

Western jewellery according to different occasions

Festive Look

Earrings

Bracelet stack

Celebration Look

Earrings

Bracelet stack

CHAPTER VIII

Day vs. Night Styling

"Adapt your jewellery choices for daytime elegance or nighttime glamour with ease."

Jewellery has the power to change the mood of your entire outfit — and knowing how to shift from daytime elegance to nighttime glamour is the key to effortlessly elevated style. The difference lies not just in sparkle and size, but in intention: day jewellery is about being subtle, clean, and refined; night jewellery is about boldness, drama, and shine.

Here's how to master both moods — and transition between them with ease.

Daytime Elegance: Understated & Effortlessly Polished

The Vibe: Light, fresh, graceful. Perfect for work, errands, brunches, or casual day dates.

Jewellery Choices:
Delicate Stud Earrings: Pearls, small diamonds, minimalist shapes.
Fine Chains: Simple gold or silver with subtle pendants or charms.
Stackable Rings: Thin bands, midi rings, or dainty gemstones.
Minimal Bracelets: Chain links, tennis-style, or bangles in clean metals.
Style Tips:
Keep it lightweight: You want comfort and ease for the whole day.
Avoid overly sparkly or heavy items: These can feel too formal under daylight.
Coordinate with neutrals or soft colours: Rose gold, silver, or brushed gold work beautifully for daytime softness.
Perfect Pairings:
Linen shirts + gold hoops
Blazer + pearl studs + watch
T-shirt + fine pendant + simple rings

Night Time Glamour: Bold, Expressive & Sparkling

The Vibe: Confident, dramatic, luxurious. Ideal for dinner parties, formal events, dates, and nights out.

Jewellery Choices:

Statement Earrings: Chandeliers, drop earrings, bold hoops, or gem-embellished designs.

Layered Necklaces or Chunky Chains: Make a neckline pop with bold textures or shine.

Cocktail Rings: Oversized stones or unique shapes that draw attention.

Sparkling Bracelets or Cuffs: Add shimmer to the wrist, especially with sleeveless or off-shoulder outfits.

Style Tips:

Let one piece shine: Go big on earrings or a necklace — not both.

Play with contrast: Dark outfits + bright jewellery = instant drama.

Don't shy away from color or sparkle: Nighttime lighting flatters rhinestones, crystals, and vibrant stones.

Perfect Pairings:

Black dress + crystal earrings

Silk blouse + chunky gold necklace

Strapless gown + statement cuff + drop earrings

How to Transition from Day to Night

If you're going from desk to dinner or brunch to cocktails, here's how to upgrade your look in minutes:

Keep in Your Bag:

A pair of bold earrings

A statement ring or necklace

A travel-sized pouch for your day jewellery

Quick Switch Ideas:

Replace small hoops with chandeliers.

Layer an extra chain onto your day necklace.

Swap your dainty studs for gemstone drops.

Add a cuff or bold bracelet to your wrist stack.

• • •

Final Note
Day and night are two different energies, and your jewellery should
reflect that. Daytime pieces are for light, movement, and subtle charm.
Nighttime calls for drama, shine, and presence. Once you learn how to shift
between the two, you'll always be dressed for the moment, no matter
where your day (or night) takes you.

CHAPTER IX

Jewellery care and storage

"Cleaning, storing, travelling with jewellery"

Jewellery is more than just decoration — it's often deeply personal, sentimental, and sometimes a significant investment. Whether it's heirloom gold passed down through generations, your favorite everyday rings, or the dainty necklace that goes with everything, taking proper care of your jewellery ensures it stays beautiful and wearable for years to come.

Let's break down the essentials of jewellery care, from cleaning to storage, to smart travel hacks — because good pieces deserve great treatment.

Why Jewellery Care Matters:

Preserves Shine and Beauty

Over time, metals tarnish and gemstones lose their sparkle. Regular care helps restore brilliance and keeps your pieces looking like new.

Prevents Damage

Proper storage prevents scratches, bending, or stone loss. This is especially important for delicate pieces and softer gems like opals or pearls.

Protects Sentimental and Monetary Value

Heirlooms, investments, or gifted jewellery often hold emotional and financial value. Caring for them is caring for the stories they carry.

Cleaning Tips: How to Keep Your Jewellery Sparkling

Daily Tips:-

Last On, First Off: Always put on your jewellery after makeup, perfume, and lotion to avoid product build-up.

Wipe Down: Use a soft, dry cloth at the end of the day to remove oils and dirt.

Special Care Notes:

Pearls: Wipe with a damp cloth; never soak.

Silver: Use anti-tarnish polish or cloth.

Taking care of silver jewellery at home is simple but essential to maintain its shine and prevent tarnishing. Always store your silver pieces in a cool, dry place—preferably in an airtight container or zip-lock bag to minimize exposure to air and moisture. You can also add a small piece of chalk, silica gel, or anti-tarnish paper in your jewellery box to absorb humidity. Avoid contact with water, perfumes, lotions, and other chemicals, as these can speed up tarnishing. After wearing, gently wipe each piece with a soft, dry cloth to remove any sweat or oils. For a deeper clean, mix a few drops of mild dish soap with warm water, soak the jewellery for a few minutes, then clean it with a soft brush and rinse thoroughly—drying it completely before storing. With regular care and a little attention, your silver jewellery will stay beautiful and bright for years to come.

Gold & Diamonds: Soak and brush gently; avoid harsh chemicals.

Costume Jewellery: Avoid soaking — use a dry brush and wipe gently.

Smart Storage Tips: Keep Jewellery Safe & Tangle-Free

Best Practices:-

Store separately: Use soft pouches or lined compartments to avoid scratches and tangles.

Avoid sunlight & moisture: Keep pieces in a cool, dry place. Humidity speeds up tarnishing.

Invest in a proper jewellery box: Choose one with compartments, velvet lining, and space for rings, chains, and earrings.

Bonus Tip:

Hang necklaces or use necklace hooks to prevent tangling.

Store fine jewellery flat and uncluttered to protect delicate settings.

Travelling with Jewellery: Stylish and Safe On-the-Go Tips

Travelling with jewellery doesn't have to mean tangled chains and lost studs. Here's how to keep your sparkle safe when you're on the move:

Travel Tips:

Use a travel jewellery case: Compact, with zipped pouches and separate compartments.

Straw trick for necklaces: Thread delicate chains through straws to avoid tangling.

Pillboxes or contact lens cases: Great for storing small items like rings or earrings.

Never pack fine jewellery in checked baggage: Always keep it in your carry-on.

Pro Travel Advice:

Only bring what you'll wear — skip sentimental or irreplaceable pieces.

Photograph what you pack — in case of loss or insurance claims.

Consider a small polishing cloth in your kit to refresh pieces before wearing.

• • •

Final Thought

Jewellery care isn't just a routine task — it's a meaningful practice that reflects how much you value your style and the stories your pieces hold. Every item in your collection, whether it's a precious heirloom passed down through generations, a gift from someone special, or a trendy piece you picked up on a whim, deserves thoughtful attention. Regular cleaning restores their natural shine, while proper storage protects them from wear and tear, ensuring they stay as stunning as the day you got them.

When you take the time to gently clean your favourite rings, detangle your necklaces, or carefully pack a pair of earrings for a trip, you're not just preserving the materials — you're preserving memories, milestones, and moments. Much like your wardrobe reflects who you are, your jewellery tells a silent story of your personality, taste, and experiences. Giving these pieces the care they deserve is not about perfection; it's about respect for their beauty, their craftsmanship, and their significance in your life.

So, whether you're sorting through your everyday staples or polishing your statement pieces, approach it with intention. Store them well, clean them often, and travel with them smartly. With a little love and maintenance, your jewellery will continue to shine — not just in its brilliance, but in the confidence and elegance it brings to your every look.

Jewelry CARE

Keep away from
moisture

Remove when
sleeping

Allow perfumes
or lotion dry
before wearing

Remove before
entering water

Store in a closed
bag or box

Remove when
active

CHAPTER X

Confidence is the Final Accessory

"Remember that the best accessory you can wear is confidence—it ties your whole look together"

You can wear the most dazzling diamonds or stack your fingers with the finest gold rings—but nothing completes a look quite like confidence. It's invisible, yet unmistakable. It doesn't sparkle, but it radiates. Confidence is the one accessory that transforms your jewellery from decoration into a true expression of self.

Jewellery, at its best, isn't about following trends or copying what others wear. It's about feeling good in what you choose to wear, owning your style, and letting every piece reflect who you are in that moment. Whether it's a bold statement necklace or a subtle silver band, it comes alive when worn with assurance.

You might have noticed it—how someone wearing a single chain with total self-belief can light up a room more than someone layered in luxury but unsure of their choices. That's the power of confidence. It's what turns fashion into style, and accessories into statements.

So how do you build that confidence?

Start with pieces that feel like you. Not what's trending—what resonates. Maybe it's a sentimental charm, a ring you never take off, or earrings that make you feel powerful.

Experiment, unapologetically. Try mixing metals, layering necklaces, or wearing bold cuffs with casual looks. When you give yourself permission to play, you'll discover new facets of your personal style.

Wear your jewellery with intention. Know what mood you're setting, what story you're telling. Jewellery has energy—and when you wear it consciously, it aligns with you.

In the end, jewellery should empower you. It should add a layer of beauty, yes—but more than that, it should amplify your presence. Whether you're walking into a room with stacked bangles that jingle with every step, or letting a single pearl pendant speak volumes in its silence, the magic happens when you wear it like you mean it.

Because no matter how curated your look, how polished your pieces, or how stunning your accessories—confidence is what ties it all together. It's the final flourish. The ultimate statement. And the one thing that never goes out of style.

Why Confidence is the Key:-

It empowers your choices: You stop dressing for approval and start dressing for yourself.

It encourages creativity: You mix metals, try new combinations, or wear that bold piece you've been saving — just because you want to.

It adds presence: When you walk into a room feeling good in your style, people notice — not just your jewellery, but your energy.

Building Style Confidence: A Personal Practice

Just like style, confidence is personal — and it's something you can grow and strengthen over time. Here's how jewellery can help:

1. Start with Meaningful Pieces

Wearing jewellery that holds personal value — a gift from a loved one, a family heirloom, or something that symbolizes an achievement — connects you to your story. That connection builds presence. When you feel emotionally rooted in what you wear, your confidence naturally follows.

2. Embrace Signature Style

Find what makes you feel like you. Maybe it's layered chains, minimalist rings, or bold statement earrings. Whatever it is, own it. Your signature pieces become part of your identity — a visual language people associate with your presence.

3. Dress for Your Mood, Not the Rules

Feeling powerful? Stack the rings and go bold. Feeling soft and romantic? Reach for dainty chains and pearls. When you honour how you feel, you show up as your most authentic self — and authenticity is the heart of confidence.

Final Reflection:-

Jewellery may sparkle, but you are the true light. A ring won't make you confident. A necklace can't make you bold. But when you wear them with clarity, pride, and purpose, they become tools of empowerment — mirrors of your energy, strength, and joy.

So the next time you're getting ready — whether it's for a big event, a casual outing, or simply another day in your life — remember this:

The most beautiful thing you can wear isn't on your neck, wrist, or ears. It's how you show up in the world.

CHAPTER XI

Jewellery Birthstone Guide by Month

"I believe that wearing your birthstone is a deeply personal choice"

It truly depends on how much you resonate with its meaning and benefits, and whether you wish to incorporate it into your everyday style. I always recommend wearing something that makes you feel like it's truly yours—something that reflects your personality and energy. When a piece of jewellery feels made for you, the connection to it becomes even more special. Styling your birthstone can be a beautiful addition to your permanent jewellery collection if you genuinely connect with it, or simply something you wear whenever it feels right. The idea is to introduce you to the stone that represents your birth month—or even your loved ones', in case you want to gift them something meaningful they'll feel truly connected to.

• • •

Birthstone Guide

January – Garnet

Deep red and richly elegant, garnet jewellery adds warmth and boldness to any look. It symbolises protection and strength, perfect for statement rings or vintage-inspired pieces.

February – Amethyst

With its calming purple hues, amethyst is ideal for chic pendants, earrings, or cocktail rings. It brings clarity, peace, and spiritual charm to your collection.

March – Aquamarine

Soft blue aquamarine works beautifully in delicate, minimal jewellery. It evokes calm, courage, and timeless sophistication—ideal for everyday wear.

April – Diamond

The ultimate classic, diamonds symbolise eternal love and power. Whether in studs, solitaire rings, or layered necklaces, they're a must-have in every jewellery box.

May – Emerald

Known for their lush green glow, emeralds stand out in gold settings. They add richness and elegance to traditional and contemporary designs.

June – Pearl (or Moonstone, Alexandrite)

Pearls offer timeless grace—perfect for minimal chains, hoops, or bridal jewellery. Moonstone adds a mystical glow, and alexandrite brings color-shifting uniqueness.

July – Ruby

Rubies bring fiery elegance and are often used in regal or bridal jewellery. Their bold red hue symbolizes love, courage, and passion.

August – Peridot

Bright green peridot pops in modern, playful jewellery styles. It symbolizes positivity and renewal, great for rings and stacked bangles.

September – Sapphire

Deep blue sapphires lend sophistication to both classic and contemporary designs. They pair beautifully with diamonds for elegant contrast.

October – Opal (or Tourmaline)

Opals dazzle with rainbow-like play of color—ideal for statement jewellery with an artistic flair. Tourmalines offer a wide color range, from pink to green, for vibrant looks.

November – Topaz (or Citrine)

Golden citrine and topaz add warmth and sparkle. These stones are perfect in boho or festive jewellery styles, symbolizing joy and abundance.

December – Tanzanite (or Blue Topaz)

Tanzanite gives a bold, earthy touch to rings, cuffs, and ethnic jewellery. Blue topaz and tanzanite are great for icy, elegant winter looks.

Birthstones

52

January

Garnet

Loyalty | Protection

February

Amethyst

Wisdom | Peace

March

Aquamarine

Courage | Tranquility

April

Diamond

Strength | Eternal Love

May

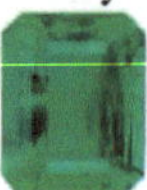

Emerald

Hope | Prosperity

June

Pearl

Purity | Femininity

July

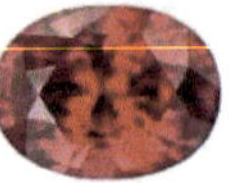

Ruby

Passion | Vitality

August

Peridot

Happiness | Protection

September

Sapphire

Wisdom| Loyalty

October

Opal

Creativity | Diversity

November

Topaz

Success | Warmth

December

Tanzanite

Luck | Balance

CHAPTER XII

Building a Capsule Jewellery Wardrobe

"Curate a timeless, versatile collection that effortlessly elevates every outfit"

A capsule jewellery wardrobe is all about quality over quantity. Just like your clothing essentials—those few pieces you reach for again and again—your jewellery capsule should include timeless, versatile items that blend seamlessly with your everyday style. Whether you're dressing for a casual coffee date, a work meeting, or a formal event, the right jewellery staples can transform your look with minimal effort.

Start by identifying your core style—do you lean toward minimalism, bold statements, or a mix of both? This helps you choose pieces that feel true to you. A well-balanced capsule should include the basics: a pair of everyday studs, a dainty necklace or two, a stackable ring set, and a classic bracelet or bangle. These items can be worn solo for subtle elegance or layered together to create a more elevated or expressive look.

Pay attention to metal tones as well—gold, silver, rose gold, or mixed metals. Choose the one that complements your skin tone and wardrobe the best. If you wear mostly neutral or warm tones, gold might be your go-to. If you wear cooler shades or prefer sleek modern aesthetics, silver or platinum may be a better fit. Don't be afraid to mix metals—this adds personality and breaks old fashion rules.

Invest in high-quality pieces that last—opt for materials like sterling silver, gold. Quality jewellery not only looks better but also becomes part of your signature style over time. And don't forget to include at least one personal or meaningful piece, such as a birthstone, engraved charm, or heirloom—it adds heart to your collection.

While fine jewellery is timeless, don't underestimate the power of costume jewellery. It allows you to experiment with bold trends, statement pieces, and playful styles without a big investment. Costume jewellery is incredibly versatile, giving you the freedom to change your look depending on your mood, outfit, or occasion. It's also lightweight and travel-friendly, making it ideal for vacations or on-the-go styling where you want variety without the stress of carrying or losing expensive items. With the right pieces, costume jewellery can offer big impact with minimal effort, proving that style doesn't always have to come with a heavy price tag.

A capsule jewellery wardrobe is about intentional styling. It gives you the power to express yourself with just a few curated pieces. You'll find that having fewer, better items expands your styling options, reduces decision fatigue, and helps you always feel polished, no matter the occasion.

You Were Born To Shine

Final Thoughts from Rashi-

As you close this book, I hope you feel something shift—not just in your jewellery box, but in the way you see yourself.

This wasn't just a guide on how to wear accessories. It was a gentle reminder that you already have everything it takes to shine. Jewellery is simply a mirror—one that reflects your mood, your energy, your story. And now, you know how to use it with intention and style.

Whether you're reaching for a delicate chain on a quiet Monday, layering bold pieces for a festive celebration, or choosing that one ring that always makes you feel powerful—do it with joy. Do it for you.

Remember, there are no fixed rules in style—only moments of truth. Trust your instinct. Play. Experiment. Be bold one day, and understated the next. Let your jewellery evolve as you do.

And whenever you need a reminder, flip back to these pages. I'll be right here.

Thank you for letting me into your world. It's been an honour to walk this journey with you.

Keep shining,

Rashi Sharma *-"Your brightest admirer"*

www.ingramcontent.com/pod-product-compliance
Lightning Source LLC
Chambersburg PA
CBHW040915110726
48005CB00006B/900